HOW TO REALLY LOVE YOUR HUSBAND

How to
Really Love
Your Husband

Love-in-Action Ideas for Every Day

H. NORMAN WRIGHT

Servant Publications
Ann Arbor, Michigan

© 1995 by H. Norman Wright
All rights reserved.

Vine Books is an imprint of Servant Publications especially designed to serve evangelical Christians.

Scripture quotations in this book have been taken from various translations of the Bible, including Holy Bible, New International Version (NIV), The New King James Version of the Bible (NKJV), and the Living Bible (LB), as noted in the text. All rights reserved.

Published by Servant Publications
P.O. Box 8617
Ann Arbor, Michigan 48107

Cover design by Hile Design and Illustration

95 96 97 98 99 10 9 8 7 6 5 4 3 2 1

Printed in the United States of America
ISBN 0-89283-885-X

Library of Congress Cataloging-in-Publication Data

Wright, H. Norman
  How to really love your husband : love-in-action ideas for everyday / H. Norman Wright.
        p.   cm.
  ISBN 0-89283-885-X
  1. Marriage—Miscellanea. 2. Love —Miscellanea. 3. Husbands—Psychology—
Miscellanea. I. Title.
HQ734.W94915 1995
248.8'435—dc20   95-12235
                                                                          CIP

1

Build your husband's self-confidence and motivate
him to action by letting him know you
need him and appreciate him.

2

Men tend to take things literally. When you ask your
husband to do something for you, phrase it with a
"Would you?" instead of a "Could you?"
He'll know you want help and aren't
just asking a hypothetical question![1]

3

What's your husband's favorite hobby? Study up
on the topic through reading, lessons, or
whatever it takes, and one day surprise
him with your knowledge and skill!

4

If your husband becomes quiet during a discussion,
don't assume he's ignoring you. Many men like to
put important issues on the back burner and think
about them before talking. Give him time.

5

When you share your feelings with your husband, let
him know you're not trying to tell him what to do—
you just want him to listen and consider how you feel.
Tell him directly, "When you listen to my
feelings I feel loved and supported."

6

Trust your husband. He needs to know you believe he wants the best for you and he is doing his best in the marriage. When you are open and receptive to what he has to offer, you fulfill his need for love. In turn, he loves back.[2]

7

Write down your husband's requests so you can
remember them without having to be reminded.
He'll notice!

8

Let your husband know ahead of time what kind of
support you want from him. You'll find it easier
to share your concerns and feelings when *you*
know *he* knows what to expect.[3]

9

Take a few minutes to freshen up and fix your face and
hair before your husband comes home from work.
He'll know you did it just for him.

10

Many men remember numbers easily: batting averages,
stock market figures, field goal percentages. Does
your husband know what you'd like him
to remember? Write down specific dates
and occasions for him as reminders.

11

Many men don't want to be bothered when they're upset or in a bad mood. Ask, "Is there something I can do to help, or would you prefer I leave you alone? I'm willing to do either."

12

When your husband asks forgiveness for an offense, let him know that you love and value as well as forgive him. True forgiveness does not depress one's self-esteem; it elevates it.

13

Reconciliation makes equals of a husband and wife.
In true reconciliation, neither is put down. Do you feel
equal in your relationship? Does your husband feel
as though you value his contributions? Ask!

14

Be direct with requests. Not: "It would really be nice
to eat out one night this week," delivered with a sigh.
Instead, simply: "Would you take me
out to dinner one night this week?"

15

Romance in marriage doesn't just happen. You can
make it happen by your attention, desire,
thoughts, and actions.

16

When was the last time you gave your husband a back
rub? Fixed his favorite dessert? Dropped by his office
in the afternoon? Called to say, "I love you and
I'm looking forward to seeing you tonight"?
Surprise him!

17

Ask your husband what two or three prayer requests
he would like to have answered in the next thirty days.
Write the requests on cards, leaving space to write in
answers, and place them where you'll both see
them every day. Rejoice with him when
his prayers are answered!

18

Praise your husband in front of others. Tuck special
notes in his shirt pocket or briefcase. A man is
much more open to change when he feels
loved, trusted, and accepted.

19

What does your husband do that makes you feel loved,
valued, and respected? Write it down and slip it into
a recent issue of his favorite magazine or tape it
to the sports page of the newspaper.

20

Your husband welcomes soothing, helpful, brief, and
sensitive communication. Ask him what time of
day is best for him to talk with you, too.

21

Pay attention when your husband talks to you. Turn
off or put away any distractions. Look him in
the eye and give him feedback. An inexpensive
but extremely valuable gift!

22

Admire your husband. Give him thanks, approval, and
appreciation. He'll feel secure in your admiration and
want to continue to meet your needs.

23

If your husband doesn't hear you when you say "I love
you," it may be that you've been saying it the same
way for too long. Say it in a way that will surprise him!
Write it on the bathroom mirror or in his daily calendar, or clip a note to the sun visor in his car.

24

It's not your job to reform your husband. Encourage
him, praise him, never take him for granted.
You can request change, but leave the work
of transformation up to the Holy Spirit.

25

Don't compete with your husband—be his friend.
Wish him the best and be enthusiastic about his
achievements. Brag about him!

26

Take on the roles of both student and teacher in your
marriage. A fulfilled marriage is one in which
husband and wife teach one another and
learn from one another.

27

Pray together often. "It is only when a husband and wife pray together before God that they find the secret of true harmony, that the difference in their tastes enriches their home instead of endangering it."[4]

28

Talk with your husband about your budget, bank accounts, and tax returns. Withholding your worries and concerns about finances only makes them greater.

29
Remember: There is no perfect husband,
perfect wife, or perfect marriage.

30
Genuine love for your husband is incompatible with
jealousy, envy, or bitterness. Those responses will push
him away rather than draw him close to you.

31
Silence is not always golden, especially between
husband and wife. Ask your husband if he'd
like to set aside time just to talk.

32
Disagreeing with your husband is one thing; behaving
disagreeably is another. Tell him that you love
him even if you don't see eye to eye.

33

Find a recording of your husband's favorite song and
play it for him. Ask him what sounds he finds most
soothing and relaxing and provide them for him.

34

Realize that sometimes your love for your husband will
be a decision instead of a strong feeling. That's
mature, lasting love. That's *agape* love.

35

When your husband is upset, exhausted, or overwhelmed, do you know what he needs most of all? It may be simple companionship. It may be space, or peace and quiet. Be there for him. Your sensitivity, presence, patience, and prayers will help him feel loved.

36

Fantasizing in marriage is healthy as long as a wife's
mind is filled with visions of her husband.
Fantasize about your husband!

37

When you love your husband, you take his feelings and
viewpoints seriously even when they differ
from your own. When you disagree, tell him,
"I see things differently, but maybe I can
learn from you." Believe it!

38

Telling your husband, "You don't understand" won't help him understand your needs better. That phrase is accusative and he won't hear it. Try, "Let me say it another way."[5]

39

Never seek guidance from God about something He has already forbidden in His Word. All we need to do is be obedient.

40
Lectures belong in the classroom, not in the home.
Sacrificial love doesn't demand; it respectfully asks.

41
Ask once; don't nag. If your husband complains,
don't argue. Let him make his own decision
in his own time.

42
Settle issues in your marriage as soon as they come up.
"Harmony in marriage exists when there is an
absence of unsettled issues and offenses
between the two of you."[6]

43
Blame in a marriage may identify responsibility, but it
does nothing to bring about reconciliation.

44
Limit your discussion of problems to one issue at a
time. Let your husband know that listening to you
may be the best part of the solution.

45
Recognize that expressing your anger is not
necessarily bad; it's *how* you express your
anger that makes the difference.

46

Intimacy in marriage is both sexual and emotional,
but emotional intimacy is the prelude to sexual
intimacy. Let your husband know that when he
gives you conversation and attention every day
of your marriage, you are able to respond to
him sexually to a greater degree.

47

For your next anniversary, give your husband a card
listing as many reasons why you're glad you
married him as years you've been married.

48

Many men resist shopping. Make it interesting for
your husband by presenting him with a map of your
favorite mall, and a list of items that would interest
him, along with a list of the stores in which
he'll find each item. He'll love it!

49
In the midst of personal or family crisis, don't waste
energy trying to figure out *why*. Trust God, use your
energy creatively, and know that solutions will follow.

50
What is God's plan for you and your family at this
time? "The will of God grows on you. That which
is not of God will die—you will lose interest.
But the plan of God will never die."[7]

51

Temptation is inevitable, but it's not the problem.
What you *do* with temptation *can* be the problem. Will
you play with it, entertain it, or evict it?

52
Talk with your husband about how you see God, who
He is, and what He is like. Ask about his viewpoint.

53
What cripples a marriage is not the problems and
conflicts, but emotional malnutrition brought
on by apathy and indifference.

54

See if you can "out-serve" your husband. Now there's a worthy competition! Think of three new ways you can serve your husband this week.

55

Know that you will make mistakes as a wife. Your husband knows it, and God does, too. Don't give up—learn from your mistakes and move on.

56

It was through the process of doing things for and with your husband that you fell in love. It's how you'll stay in love. Send the kids out to a baby-sitter, have a bubble bath waiting for your husband when he gets home, share a picnic dinner in front of the fireplace. Be wild and creative!

57

Do whatever you can to help your husband feel accepted. A husband who feels secure in his role responds to his wife with love.

58

Does your husband know you well enough to write your biography from age one to fifteen? If not, help him out. You'll generate a great discussion, and he'll understand you better.

59
Treating your husband in loving ways is like putting money in a savings account. It pays interest. Make plenty of deposits!

60
When your husband lets you know you've hurt or offended him, think about your goal and choose your response. Will you be defensive? Resentful? Humble? Sorrowful? If your goal is to be close again, the choice is clear.

61
Before making love with your husband some evening,
read aloud from the Song of Solomon.

62
What dreams do you have for your marriage that are
still unrealized? Share them with your husband and
create an opportunity for them to unfold.

63
What three questions or phrases would your husband like you to drop from your vocabulary? If you don't know, ask. Then do it!

64
The words "If only..." stop action and create unnecessary worry and a sense of uneasiness in your marriage. When you feel an "If only" coming on, say instead, "Let's commit this to the Lord."

65

What gift would your husband never expect from you?
Don't ask him. Figure it out for yourself, then
give it. Watch a new image of you develop
in his heart and mind.

66

Before giving your husband advice, ask if he wants it.
He may just need you to accept his words in silence.

67

Allow your husband to be unique. "That's just like a
man!" or "You men are all the same!" does nothing to
promote understanding.

68

Differences between you and your husband can either
drive you apart and weaken your marriage, or they can
help you develop a strength you would never
experience any other way. List three ways you
and your husband are different and consider
how each difference might strengthen
your marriage.

69

Help your husband think about and fulfill his potential. Ask him, "What do you want to be doing five years from now? Ten years from now? How can I help you achieve those things?"

70

Working out a disagreement with your husband? Attack the problem rather than the person. Suggest alternatives rather than stubbornly sticking to your solution as though it's the only one.

71
Be willing to do some things the way your husband
does them. Organize the tools in the garage his way, or
put the mail next to his chair instead of on the kitchen
table, just to please him.

72
Purchase a dozen Valentine's Day cards in February
and send one to your husband each month of the year.

73
When you have an important decision to make, first
pray for wisdom, then ask your husband for his input.
Keep in mind that he may know best!

74

"If you refuse criticism you will end in poverty and disgrace; if you accept criticism you are on the road to fame" (Proverbs 13:18 LB). What accurate criticism has your husband voiced recently that you haven't accepted? Admit it to yourself and to him.

75
"If you love someone you will be loyal to him no
matter what the cost. You will always believe
in him, always expect the best of him, and
always stand your ground in defending him"
(1 Corinthians 13:7 LB).

76

Don't look at your marital woes through a telephoto lens, focusing just on the problems. Balance your perspective. List all the positives about your marriage and share them with your husband.

77

Pray, study Scripture, or read devotional materials with your husband on a regular basis. The closer you are to God, the easier it will be for you to be open to your husband.

78

Don't assume you know what your husband is think-
ing when he's silent. Tell him, "There's no way
I can know what you're thinking right now, but
I'd like to know. I promise if you decide to
share with me I'll just listen without comment."
Then keep your part of the bargain!

79
Leave a note on the dashboard of your husband's car
asking how you could be a better listener. Thank him
for his suggestions and put them into practice.

80
It's far easier to avoid conflict in marriage than to take
steps necessary to resolve conflict. Avoidance,
however, will only complicate matters. To make
conflicts disappear, face them, discuss them,
and look for creative ways to resolve them.

81

To what extent are you irresistible to your husband?
To what extent are the two of you still incompatible?
Are you moving from incompatibility to irresistibility?
Think of three ways to reduce your incompatibility,
increase your irresistibility, or both.

82
Forgiveness is not a paid-up life insurance policy.
It needs continual investment for
a marriage renewal policy.

83

Frustrated when your husband doesn't talk to you?
Practice patience and acknowledge his efforts at
communication. Express appreciation when he
listens to you, listen without interruption
when he does talk, and don't pressure him
for more. Eventually he'll share more with you.

84

"A word fitly spoken is like apples of gold in settings of silver" (Proverbs 25:11 NKJV). The translation for marriage: "The right word at the right time, how good it is!" When is the right time for you to talk to your husband?

85
List the experiences in your marriage so far that you
will want to remember twenty-five years from
now. Ask your husband to create a similar
list and share it with you.

86
Make the following vow to your husband: "Neither by
day nor by night will I ever cut you down in company.
Not before my family, your family, our family."[8]

87

The quality of your spiritual life will be the remedy for the aches and pains dispensed by life's stresses. Discuss your shared spiritual life on a regular basis. Talk about how you could make it even better.

88

If your lines of communication need repair, be your own handyman. You and your husband may need to tear down some walls before you can rebuild the relationship. Set aside ten minutes every day for uninterrupted talk. It's a beginning.

89

Remember that in a marriage the question is not so
much who is right, but what is right for the
marriage. Think about it.

90

A loving wife calls her husband's strengths to his attention and helps him discover and develop his potential. Make a list of your husband's strengths. Ask him to do the same for you and then share your lists. Let him know you believe in him.

91
Work hard at making yourself understood. Ask questions, give examples, repeat your responses, use words and illustrations your husband can identify with. Focus on visual examples.

92
Invite your husband to a romantic rendezvous by making a cassette or home video tape. Have fun with it! Play it for him in a private moment. He'll appreciate your creativity!

93

"I delight in your decrees; I will not neglect your word" (Psalm 119:16 NIV). Do you have a regular pattern for memorizing scripture? If not, suggest to your husband that you memorize a verse together every two weeks.

94

"High blood pressure in marriage is caused by fat clogging the veins of communication."⁹

95

Are you predictable? Do you always follow the same
routine? Make something new happen in your
relationship with your husband today.
Go ahead—surprise him!

96

Stress tends to make men quiet, withdrawn, or irritable. Avoid giving your husband advice when he's feeling stressed; instead, offer him space, a listening ear, a gentle hug, or the reassurance of lovemaking.

97

In marriage, we must cherish the ability to let loose in
reckless displays of affection and admiration.[10]

98

One of the greatest gifts you can give your husband is
the right to fail and to be imperfect. After all, it's
what *you* want from *him*, isn't it?

99

If you think you've made some positive changes your
husband has requested, evaluate them with *his*
measuring stick as well as your own. Ask him
what he thinks. Don't argue with his answer.

100

Have you ever told your husband, "You make me so
angry"? Does he really have that much power over
you? Is there another possibility? Think about it.

101

Loving your husband means recognizing specific needs and offering to meet them. Be sure to meet his needs in the way he'd like you to. If you're unsure, ask.

102

Instead of complaining to others about your marriage,
tell your husband what you *do* like about your
marriage and make positive suggestions for
making it even better.

103

Listening to your husband means you're not thinking about your response while he's still talking (Proverbs 18:13). When he finishes talking, summarize what he said to make sure you understood.

104
Instead of buying an anniversary card this year, write
your own and have it printed on parchment paper.
Have it delivered to your husband in an unusual way: a
business associate, a neighbor, the family dog!

105

What is your plan for ongoing maintenance and renewal of your marriage? This year, read a marriage enhancement book together or attend a marriage class or seminar. He'll love it if you make all the arrangements.

106

All wives offend their husbands at some point. Some
are oblivious to their husband's hurt, some ignore it,
and some admit their offense and ask forgiveness.
What has been your pattern? Practice asking
forgiveness. It will draw you closer together.

107

On a scale of 0 to 10, where would you rate your marriage today? Where would your husband rate it? Predict his answer and then ask him.

108

Remember that love isn't an act; it's a way of life. It's being there during good times and not-so-good times. Being there is always possible when Jesus is invited to be there, too.

109

Does the TV in your home build your marriage relationship or detract from it? Ask your husband if he would agree to keep the television off for a month so you can work on your communication with each other.

110

Marriage often turns out to be more than you expected. But you and your husband can shape the future of your marriage by determining its direction. List three common goals you and your husband have for your marriage. If you don't have any, don't wait any longer!

111

Make it your business to know at least five of your
husband's needs and how to meet those needs
in a way he desires. Most men, for example,
have a need for admiration. It would be
difficult to give too many compliments!

112
The marriage relationship is God's way of reflecting his eternal love for his people. What priority should we give to it? What priority do you give to it?

113
Listen for God's voice. "And if you leave God's paths and go astray, you will hear a Voice behind you say, 'No, this way; walk here'" (Isaiah 30:21 LB).

114

God does not quit on us. A wife's wedding vows to her husband are a reflection of God's pledge to never leave us and never give up on us. What area of your marriage could use more attention and effort?

115
Have you ever thought about what your husband
might look like twenty years from now, or
what you might look like? Talk with him
about your thoughts.

116

Be careful what you say to your husband in anger.
Never say anything that reflects on his abilities or
diminishes who he is as a person. Hurt that comes
from angry words can last long after you've forgotten
what your anger was all about.

117

Men are quite sensitive to criticism. Think positive: give your husband suggestions and time to think about them rather than a negative "Why did you do that?" or "I know a better way to do it."

118

Being your husband's friend means encouraging him
to reach his potential and delighting in his success
as if you had just won the Miss America contest.
Think of a personal goal your husband has
recently achieved and plan a celebration
with a few close friends.

119

Change is a vital part of a growing marriage. List three
ways you are different this year compared to last. Ask
your husband what he thinks.

120

Think of two or three recent times you've shared with
your husband feelings of failure, sadness, or
disappointment. If you can't, today's a
new day. Let him see you as you are.

121

Make a list of your needs and ask God to show you which are important. Let Him decide. Better to lead a God-centered life than a need-centered life.

122

Forgiveness in marriage is tied to grace rather than justice. It lets your husband off the hook. It doesn't make him pay again and again for the same failure. Forgive and forget.

123
Failing doesn't make you a failure in your
marriage. Giving up, withdrawing, viewing
yourself as a failure, and refusing to learn
from your experience might!

124
Tell your husband that he's more important to
you than work or household tasks—then
find some way to prove it to him!

125
Friendship between a husband and wife is rated as the number one reason for marital happiness. Having a close friendship comes from *being* a good friend. Laughing, playing, talking, and working together builds friendship.

126
"The more important a man feels he is to his wife,
the more he encourages her to do the
activities he knows she enjoys."[11]

127
On a scale of 0 to 10, how important are your
possessions to you? "Then [Jesus] said to them,
'Watch out! Be on your guard against all
kinds of greed; a man's life does not
consist in the abundance of his possessions'"
(Luke 12:15 NIV).

128

Remember you don't need to look for guidance in the
areas where God has already said "Yes" and has
given a command. All you need is to be obedient.[12]
Should you love your husband?
No question!

129

When a woman loves her husband, she opens herself up to a new level of hurt. But understand that when a man doesn't feel loved or respected by his wife, the pain of rejection is intense. Take the risk. Tell your husband daily that you love and appreciate him.

130

The next time you are sick, notice how you act with
your husband. Are you pleasant or unapproachable?
Are you easy to take care of or should you be
confined to an isolation ward?! Your husband
may be able to tell you.

131

A wife doesn't *have* to submit to her husband, care for him, help him. She *gets* to! Tell your husband you've learned it's a privilege to love him. Ask how you can help him even more.

132

"The only time to stop temptation is at the point of recognition. If one begins to argue and engage in a hand-to-hand combat, temptation almost always wins the day."[13]

133
Women often relate to God in one of four ways: "Give me," "Use me," "Make me," or "Search me, O God, and know my heart." Where are you today?

134
Don't let the sun go down on your anger.
Resolve your differences as soon as possible—
a great idea in marriage.

135

A 50/50 marriage doesn't work; it's too hard
to figure out if you and your husband have
both come halfway. With a 100/100
commitment, there isn't a question.

136

Tell your husband how you see God working in your lives. "Unless the Lord builds the house, its builders labor in vain" (Psalm 127:1 NIV).

137
Remind yourself often that wives who give a little
love find it goes a long way, and wives who give
a lot of love find it just keeps going and
going and going forever.

138
Tell your husband on a regular basis, "I love you more than yesterday and less than tomorrow."

139
Write your husband a note telling him he's a memorable person and why.[14]

140
The next time you find yourself arguing with
your husband, ask yourself, "Is my goal to
punish and dominate my husband, or
to understand him?" If needed, redirect
your arguments toward the
goal of reconciliation.

141
Romance is like a coal that needs your breath
and patience to ignite. If you want a stronger
marriage, take a few breaths and blow!

142
Your husband has a love bank. Every time you interact
with him you make a deposit or a withdrawal.
Have you checked the ledger lately?
Keep those books balanced![15]

143
When a wife gives her husband second place—because
she gives her work, children, or some other interest
first place—he has three choices. He can accept second
place, press for first place and eventually win, or
press for first place until he loses heart.
Why put him through that?[16]

144

Ask your husband how the way you handle frustration
or express anger makes him feel and how it affects
your marriage. Do you draw him closer or
push him away? Ask him how you could
express those feelings differently.

145

A quality wife is one who can satisfy one man all her life long—and who can be satisfied by one man all her life long. It takes effort, time, commitment, and the grace of God, but it's possible. Make this your goal for the life of your marriage.

146

If your marriage seems dull, perhaps it's you! Maybe
you're stuck in your routine. Maybe you're too
predictable. Shock your husband! Be unusually
creative and totally unpredictable. Fix him
new meals, dress differently, sit on his lap....

147

If it takes time for you to recover from a quarrel
with your husband, that's all right. Healing can't
be rushed. But remember that his sense of timing
is different from your own. If he seems to
recover more quickly than you, it doesn't
mean he's insensitive or he didn't really
care about the issue. Give him the
benefit of the doubt.

148

"Instead of focusing on our mates—how much is
lacking—let's look at ourselves and the size of the
debt God has forgiven us. Surely He bears
with our failings. Let us commit to bear
with each other's failings when we are
weak and build each other up."[17]

149

Think about the time you spend working, whether at home or in a job setting. Tell your husband what your work means to you and what you would like to be doing in your work ten years from now.

150

Talk with your husband on an ongoing basis about
how both you and he would like your marriage to
be different. Listen without defensiveness. Take
time out to think about his ideas and yours,
and come back to the discussion later.

151

So you're on your way somewhere and your husband
is lost! Instead of pointing it out and demanding that
he stop for directions, try one of these alternatives:
"What do you want to do?" "Can I do something
to help?" "I don't mind being late. Want to
make this a wild adventure?!"

152

When your husband walks in the door after work, how
is he greeted? To what do you give your immediate
attention? Your husband wants to be Number One.
Before you do anything else, greet him with
affection and genuine interest: "I've missed you,"
"It's good to see you," "Tell me about your day."
Don't hit him with problems, negatives, or
"Do you know what *your* kids did today?!"
until he's had a chance to unwind.

153

A husband and wife who are friends don't attempt to control or dominate one another. Respect your husband's ideas and feelings. Ask often, "What do you think?" Say often, "Let's try it your way."

154

The love-talk that a couple shares before marriage is too often, after marriage, replaced by other kinds of communication. Take time to reflect, then list the things you used to talk about. Ask your husband to do the same. Introduce those topics back into your conversations.

155
Encourage your husband in specific ways. A man who
knows his wife supports him will trust her more
and be more open.

156
Talking may not be everything, but it sure beats avoiding important issues. Avoidance causes problems to
grow. When you find yourself avoiding your husband,
ask yourself, "What is our disagreement?
How can we resolve it?"

157

Conflict can open as many doors as it closes in a marriage. When you allow it to open a door between you and your husband, you'll see your differences disappear. What are some things you can do to resolve some of your differences? Think about it and come up with a list of ideas.

158
Ask your husband how you could be better at loving
and serving him. Be ready to hear his answer.
Thank him for his suggestions.

159
Love in marriage says, "Will you forgive me for the
hurt I've caused you?" When have you said this?
Do you need to say it now?

160

When a husband and wife talk about their thoughts
and feelings with each other, every problem is
diminished and every joy expanded. Share
often, but for best results, be brief.

161
"Sex is a God-ordained means of assuring your partner that he is the most important person in the world right here, right now." Make it creative, romantic, and sensitive to your husband's needs and timing.[18]

162
When your husband left for work this morning,
did he feel supported and built up by
having been home? Ask!

163
Lines open to God are invariably open to one another,
for a woman cannot be genuinely open to God
and closed to her mate.[19]

164
When you love and support the best in your husband,
many of the things that irritate you either disappear
or don't bother you as much.

165

When you find yourself arguing with your husband,
stop yourself and listen to him. Then respond with,
"If I understand your position, you are saying…"
and restate what you heard. When you stop to
consider both sides of an issue, you'll be
amazed how marital discord diminishes.

166

When your husband has had a bad day, the best words
you can say are, "I believe in you, and so does God.
What can I do to make the rest of your day easier?"

167

Who hears about it when you're upset with your husband? Nobody? Your mother? Your friends? Next time, let him know directly but calmly that you are upset, what you would like him to do differently, and that you know he is capable of it.

168
Farm out the kids and have a romantic interlude in the
living room or family room. He'll love it!

169
When your husband is struggling with a problem,
ask if he wants suggestions before giving them.
If he does, give them gently and lovingly.
Be aware of your tone of voice.

170

Go to the library and check out a book of romantic
poems. Ask your husband to select one and read it to
you just before bedtime some evening.

171

Sex and verbal communication cannot be separated.
One is not a substitute for the other. But remember
that for most men sex is a form of communication.
Lovemaking helps your husband feel accepted.

172
Scripture teaches us to praise God (Psalm 100:4) and others (Ephesians 4:29). Think of three ways you've praised your husband recently.

173
Keep in mind that love is concern for what concerns your husband. If he doesn't tell you what his concerns are, make up a list of twenty or thirty common concerns and ask him to check off several.

174
A hug or caress along with your words will make your
husband feel more understood and accepted,
especially when he's tired.

175
Come up with a list of gifts you *think* your husband
would like to receive from you. Show him the list
and ask his opinion. How well did you do?
Give him one of his choices this week.

176

Want your husband to make some kind of change?
He'll be more open if the change makes sense to
him, he doesn't feel blamed for not doing it
right, he finds that it works, and he
receives reinforcement for it from you.[20]

177
If you think of your husband as uncommunicative, try
thinking of him as precise and to the point instead.
Learn something new from his directness
and ability to condense!

178

Marriage is the best place to alter bad habits or offensive behaviors. Has your husband ever mentioned any to you? Ask him if there's anything you do he would prefer you didn't do.

179

Instead of criticizing your husband for leaving his clothes on the floor, thank him when he remembers to hang them up.

180

Be patient before God when the road seems long.
"But those who wait on the Lord shall renew their
strength; they shall mount up with wings like eagles,
they shall run and not be weary. They shall walk
and not faint" (Isaiah 40:31 NKJV).

181

Feeling trapped? When everyone in your life is demanding a piece of you and there isn't enough to go around, slip away for a quiet conversation with someone you know will just listen. How about God?

182
If your work, abilities, or attractiveness were taken
away from you for the next six months, how
would you feel about yourself? Discuss this
question with your husband sometime.

183

"A generous man will prosper; he who refreshes others
will himself be refreshed" (Proverbs 11:25 NIV). List
the ways that you are generous toward your husband.
Time? Housework? Money? How else?

184
Would you like to discover the will of God for your marriage? Go before God together. Ask Him what He wants for your marriage and determine to do it!

185
"If we wait until we have resolved every doubt, every question, before following God, we will never do anything with our life. We must step out by faith."[21]

186
Be conscious of your prayer requests. Are your
prayers compatible with the character of God
or would He violate His nature by giving
you what you're asking for?[22]

187

Develop an early warning system to combat temptation in your life. Pray together with your husband
every day. Memorize 1 Corinthians 10:13 together.

188

How does your husband know that you really care for
him? List three specific ways. If you don't know, ask.
Then ask, "How else would you like to be cared for?"

189

Talk to your husband *when* you're upset, not after the fact. Spell it out for him. He may not be as intuitive as you are, and he certainly can't read your mind!

190

In one of your braver moments, ask your husband for three things you could improve on. Tell him you respect his judgment and you'd like his help in becoming a better wife.

191

Give your husband permission to say "No" when you ask for his help or support. He'll be more open to responding to your next request.[23]

192

Love can die when a husband and wife forget how to talk to each other, when they don't make time for romance.[24] Surprise your husband this week with a romantic evening you plan yourself.

193

Write your husband a note that says, "You just go on getting better every day!"[25] Tape it to the mirror in the bathroom.

194

The best way to tell your husband about something you don't like is to tell him about something you *do* like. For example: "I really appreciate it when you call to tell me you're going to be late."

195

"When our mates have strengths we should affirm
them, but never pressure them to perform. To
criticize our mates at the point of their strength
is to kill their courage."[26]

196

Are you pressuring your husband to spend more time
at work to make more money? Think about having
him spend that time with the family instead. You may
not accumulate as many things, but investing in
lives pays great dividends.

197
An inexpensive gift that gives a thousand percent
return is an activities calendar with "Special Husband
Time" written on several days of each month.

198
Talk to your husband about his thoughts and concerns
about your marriage. Learn to see life through his eyes
as well as your own. He may see things you miss.

199

Some wives fail to contribute to their husband's happiness, some actively contribute to his unhappiness, and some make him feel like the most important man on earth. How does your husband feel?

200

Take your husband away for a romantic weekend. Tell him in advance you will not think or talk about projects at home or the kids, you won't discuss problems, and you won't hide your nose in a book. Be his servant for the weekend.

201

Reflect on the ways you communicated with your husband in the early days of your courtship. How did two strangers become intimate friends? Did you discuss dreams, goals, your faith, hobbies? Think of three ways you communicate with him now that keeps your intimacy alive. If you can't, ask him for feedback.

202

Don't assume you know what your husband is going to say before he says it. Assumptions lead to distortions, so listen carefully. He may surprise you!

203

Forgive truly. "Forgiving" your husband only if he promises never to fail again is not forgiveness. True forgiveness trusts and believes in the one you love.

204

Overlook your husband's shortcomings, but never overlook his potential! Let him know you believe in him. Ask how you can help him reach his goals.[27]

205

Husbands and wives comfort one another in time of need. How does your husband like you to comfort him? Don't guess about this—ask if you don't know. How do you prefer him to comfort you? Tell him.

206
Teach your husband gently. Use positive modeling,
gentle prodding, encouraging words.
Let him know you believe in him.

207
Be teachable. Listen to your husband, learn from his
positive modeling, accept his gentle prodding.
He believes in you!

208

If you haven't already, you will experience the death of
a parent, a close friend, a child, or your spouse. Now is
the time to think about how you will handle it.
Talk with your husband about it.

209

Your husband married you because he believed the
wonderful, attentive way you responded to him in
courtship would continue and increase after marriage.
Is that kind of response still there and growing,
or do you need to recommit?

210

Give your husband permission to grumble when you ask him to do something for you. Grumbling means he's considering your request—better than an outright "No!" Give him time. It's okay.[28]

211

When you bring up a problem or concern with your husband, tell him the bottom line first. He will be more apt to hear the rest of the details.

212
Whenever you think, "I should have listened to him,"
let your husband know. He will appreciate your
acknowledgment that he was right.

213
Tape-record a week's worth of family dinner conversations. When you play back the tape, listen to your tone
of voice. What are you communicating that you didn't
realize you were? Concentrate on *how* you say things
as well as what you say.

214

Recognize that the responsibility of the marriage is not yours alone and behave accordingly. Share the responsibility with your husband, and let him know you are sharing it. Ask him to plan six special dates for the year. Tell him you'd be thrilled if he would select a book on communication or sex and read it to you.

215

Be a sensitive listener. Give your husband feedback to let him know you're listening, but avoid interrupting or correcting him.

216

Ask your husband which of your emotional responses
he has the most difficulty accepting. Ask how he
would prefer you to respond, thank him for the
suggestion, and consider what he has to say.

217

If your husband uses a day-by-day calendar, "borrow"
it to write a personal message of love on the first
and fifteenth of each month.

218
In your marital disagreements, do you take the role of
solution-finder or fault-finder? Only one role allows
both you and your husband to be winners.
Fixing blame isn't it!

219
Listen to your husband. Sit down, stop what you're
doing, and really *listen*. It's the only way to
find out what's important to him.

220

Things aren't working the way you want them to in your marriage? Identify what you need, relate it to your husband's interests, and share a little at a time to keep his curiosity stimulated.[29]

221

"Marriage is not so much finding the right person as it is *being* the right person."[30] Are you the wife you wanted to be when you married? If not, it's still possible to become that woman.

222
Show your husband you appreciate both the big and
little things he does for you. Otherwise
he might feel discouraged.

NOTES

1. John Gray, *Men Are from Mars and Women Are from Venus* (New York: Harper Collins, 1992), 253, adapted.

2. Gray, 135, adapted.

3. John Gray, *What Your Mother Didn't Tell You and Your Father Didn't Know* (New York: Harper Collins, 1994), 157, adapted.

4. Paul Tournier, *The Healing of Persons* (New York: Harper and Row, 1965), 88-89.

5. Gray, *What Your Mother Didn't Tell You and Your Father Didn't Know,* 164, adapted.

6. Gary Smalley, *For Better or For Best* (Grand Rapids, Mich.: Zondervan, 1979), 75, adapted.

7. David Wilkerson, *I'm Not Mad at God* (Minneapolis: Bethany Fellowship, 1967), 32.

8. Charlie Shedd, *Letters to Philip* (Old Tappan, N.J.: Revell, 1968), 64.

9. James R. Bjorge, *Forty Ways to Say I Love You* (Minneapolis: Augsburg, 1978), 59-60.

10. Bjorge, 24.

11. Smalley, 47.

12. A.W. Tozer. Adapted, source unknown.

13. Thomas à Kempis.

14. Shedd, 31.

15. Willard F. Harley, Jr. *His Needs, Her Needs* (Grand Rapids, Mich.: Revell, 1986), 13.

16. Patrick M. Morley, *Two Part Harmony* (Nashville: Nelson, 1994), 79, adapted.

17. Morley, 143.

18. Charlie Shedd, *Letters to Karen* (Nashville: Abingdon, 1965), 111.

19. Dwight Small, *After You Say I Do* (Grand Rapids, Mich.: Revell, 1968), 214.

20. Gray, *What Your Mother Didn't Tell You and Your Father Didn't Know,* 263, adapted.

21. Richard Exley, *The Making of a Man* (Tulsa, Okla: Honor, 1993), 141.

22. Exley, 173, adapted.

23. Gray, *Men Are from Mars and Women Are from Venus,* 264, adapted.

24. James Dobson, *Dr. Dobson Answers Your Questions* (Wheaton, Ill.: Tyndale, 1982), 329.

25. Shedd, *Letters to Philip,* 33.

26. Morley, 143.

27. Bjorge, 30, adapted.

28. Gray, *Men Are from Mars and Women Are from Venus,* 266, adapted.

29. Smalley, 48.

30. Shedd, *Letters to Karen,* 13.